Keto Snacks:

The Powerful Benefits of Ketosis | Amazing Keto Snacks Recipes | Low Carb Keto Snacks for Every Day!

© Copyright by Chantel Stephens 2019 - All rights reserved.

The content contained within this book may not be reproduced, duplicated or transmitted without direct written permission from the author or the publisher.

Under no circumstances will any blame or legal responsibility be held against the publisher, or author, for any damages, reparation, or monetary loss due to the information contained within this book. Either directly or indirectly.

Legal Notice:

This book is copyright protected. This book is only for personal use. You cannot amend, distribute, sell, use, quote or paraphrase any part, or the content within this book, without the consent of the author or publisher.

Disclaimer Notice:

Please note the information contained within this document is for educational and entertainment purposes only. All effort has been executed to present accurate, up to date, and reliable, complete information. No warranties of any kind are declared or implied. Readers acknowledge that the author is not engaging in the rendering of legal, financial, medical or professional advice. The content within this book has been derived from various sources. Please consult a licensed professional before attempting any techniques outlined in this book.

By reading this document, the reader agrees that under no circumstances is the author responsible for any losses, direct or indirect, which are incurred as a result of the use of information contained within this document, including, but not limited to, — errors, omissions, or inaccuracies.

Table Of Contents

Disclaimer......6

Introduction......8

Ketosis......13

    What Is Ketosis?

    How Can You Induce It? The Main Features of a Keto Diet

    Benefits of Ketosis

The Benefits of a Ketogenic Diet......34

    What is a Ketogenic Diet?

    Ketosis and Ketones:

    The Physical Benefits of a Ketogenic Diet

The Benefits of Keto Snacks for your Ketogenic Diet......45

    Keto Grocery List

Low Carb Keto Snack Recipes......51

    Let's Cook!

    Zero Carb Keto Snacks

Pre- and Post-Workout Keto Snack Recipes......82

Conclusion......98

Bibliography......101

Disclaimer

Please note that the recipes provided in this book are presented as guidance, and following them step by step may still not guarantee any health benefits, weight loss, or cures, as each body is unique. The quantities presented in the recipes may work for a particular segment of the population, but in order to work for your body, you may need to consult a physician, and/or a nutritionist. These recipes can be implemented in a subjective manner, so the outcome of the diet may be influenced by the way the recipes are interpreted and implemented. The ketogenic diet may not be for everyone, so before attempting to follow this diet, please consult a specialist first, as you need to find out if this meal plan is suitable for you.

If you have or suspect that you have any food allergies, you need to consult a physician or a nutritionist, as some you may be allergic to some of the ingredients presented in this book. Also, if you have a physical condition that doesn't allow for any carbohydrate deprivation meals, then perhaps the ketogenic diet is not for you.

By reading this book, the reader agrees that the

book can't make any health or cure claims, as the results of the ketogenic diet can be influenced not only by the quality and quantity of ingredients, but also on the way the recipes are cooked.

Introduction

Today, there are many health conditions caused by the food we eat, as most people are having difficulty finding or affording high-quality food. Most of the food we eat today is processed, having little to no nutritional value. Most food types "touched" by man are more or less harmful to the human body, riddled with preservatives or other chemicals. Vegetables are grown using artificial fertilizers and special formulas to grow faster and bigger, animals are being fed concentrated food for the same reasons (to grow bigger and faster before being slaughtered), chemical toxins are used on fruits or vegetables to keep insects away. We are literally fed poison, and it's no wonder that we are so sick today.

The agitated and stressful way of life we lead in the modern era also doesn't leave us much time to have proper meals during the day. This is how the concept of fast-food was invented and developed. We are so exposed to this kind of food and other forms of processed food that we find it very difficult to get real food that can cover our basic nutritional needs.

Today's food is oriented to have more calories

than nutrients, mostly because it has too many carbohydrates, which are the primary source of glucose, the default energy source the body uses. Now, we are stuffing our face with high-calorie and high-carb food, but we still don't have enough energy to get through the day. That's why we need caffeine, soft drinks, sweets, and energy drinks to make it through the day. Consuming such food makes you feel more tired than energized, though, because the energy comes not from consuming food that is rich in glucose, it comes from burning this substance.

Due to laziness, or just lack of time, the modern-day human lives a passive and sedentary lifestyle, without much physical exercise. Physical exercise should activate the body to burn the glucose, but in most cases, it doesn't burn it completely, and the excess glucose gets stored in your blood. Massive glucose intake is too much for your insulin to handle, so it simply can't do its job (regulating the blood sugar level) when it notices too much glucose. The accumulation of glucose in your blood is the first step towards diabetes and other diseases of the heart, liver, and kidneys. Medication has been invented for plenty of these conditions in today's world, but the actual healing is still done by your body. Medicine can encourage your body to act, or it can simply mask the symptoms of a disease.

The good news is that the body can repair itself without the need for medicine in some cases, but through a special kind of diet, consisting of more natural and organic food, rich in fats and very low on carbs. By restricting your carb intake, you teach your body to forget about glucose and run on a different type of energy source: its own fat stores.

Processed food is calorie dense and is far from being a nutritious type of food. That's why you easily get hungry after eating it, so you crave more processed food, more glucose. It becomes like a drug addiction, and you need to take serious measures to fight it. Carb deprivation, or eliminating food completely will make your body burn the glucose you just had until it runs out. At that point, you will definitely feel hungry, but drastic times call for drastic measures. You will need to ignore the hunger and make sure you don't eat anything at all, or if you eat, you will have food with a minimal amount of carbs.

This practice will activate the metabolic state of ketosis, during which the body is looking for an alternative energy source, as the glucose is running out, and the insulin levels are changing. Insulin gets reactivated and starts to lower the glucose from your blood, thus regulating the blood sugar. By this time, the body is learning to use the fat cells as an alternative energy source. Meanwhile, ketones are being multiplied, and they will be used to break down the fat cells and release the energy from those fat stores.

When your body successfully runs on fats and ketones, the keto adaptation process has taken place. It can last for a longer time, depending on the method you used to induce ketosis. Intermittent fasting is one of the quickest ways to activate ketosis because you are simply not eating for a longer period of time. Usually, 12 hours after your last meal, the body will enter into the fasted state, at the same time entering ketosis. It starts to run on the energy released from breaking down your fat tissue, a process called *autophagy*.

However, your body can also run on the fats you eat, as well as the ones stored in your body. The fats you eat are more easily burned if the body engages in intense physical exercise. By trying a high-fat and low-carb diet, you can make sure your body only runs on fats. Think of it as the "biofuel" for your body. Ketosis can also be achieved through this kind of diet, called the *ketogenic* diet, or *keto* for short.. It triggers the same functions as intermittent fasting, without having to shun food completely.

The benefits of the ketogenic diet are myriad, and you can learn about them by reading this book. You can also find important information about the metabolic state of ketosis, how to induce it, and also details related to the food and drinks you can consume and those you need to avoid when going keto. This book also provides many detailed recipes of keto foods and snacks, which have been proven to have a positive impact on your health and well-being and can help you lose weight while feeling great. Happy reading!

Ketosis

What Is Ketosis?

Where does "keto" come from? This is probably the first question on everybody's mind when they stumble upon this term for the first time. It comes from a metabolic state, called *ketosis*, characterized by the use of ketones and burning fats, instead of glucose, for fuel. One of the biggest problems people face today is their addiction to carbs (short for carbohydrates), which can be found namely in processed food, but also in grain, potatoes, rice, pasta, and bread, so in perhaps the most common and popular types of foods. Since we are so overly exposed to processed food, we are most likely to eat too many carbs, far more than our bodies need. The problem with these kinds of foods is they are too rich in carbs, compared to other macronutrients like proteins. Most types of processed foods can't cover the nutritional daily requirements in a balanced way, so your body feels compelled to overeat to make up for this nutritive deficit. This kind of food is *calorie* dense, instead of being *nutrient* dense. So it has too many calories compared to the nutritional value it offers. This means that you quickly get hungry again, and your body craves more carbs. It is a vicious cycle, but it is one you can break.

Carbohydrates are the main source of glucose, which is the body's primary energy source. Since most of the people today consume excessive amounts of carbs, they end up with high levels of glucose to use for energy. The big problem is that the stored glucose is not able to be totally consumed because of a sedentary way of life, or because of the high levels of it that the body could never utilize. Guess what happens with excessive glucose? It gets stored in your blood, raising the blood sugar and insulin level. This leads to, you guessed it, diabetes and also other heart, kidney or liver diseases. These kinds of health conditions are so "popular" today, and we have to "thank" processed food and carbs for that.

What needs to be done in order to prevent or reverse such conditions? Researchers have found an answer by "digging" in the past, analyzing what kind of foods and eating habits humans had centuries or even thousands of years ago. This is how they discovered some solutions for this developing problem that is reaching epidemic levels in many countries around the world.

Not eating for a longer period of time may have a whole chain of positive impacts on your body in this case, as it can make you get rid of the glucose and excess fat. Refraining from food is a practice known nowadays as *fasting*. It's practiced for religious reasons for some people, and for health reasons for others. It's long been believed to be a procedure of detoxing and self-cleaning. Extensive studies have been conducted on this procedure and many have found that fasting can lead to incredible benefits for your body. The process of alternating a fasting period (in which you don't eat at all) with a feeding period is called *intermittent fasting*, and it's a process designated to get rid of your extra fat and to improve your health as well. By depriving yourself of food, you will force the body to use the remaining glucose and then switch to an alternative type of fuel: fats. Just think about it: You stop feeding your body for a period, but it will still need the energy to function. It will use the glucose it has available, as the glucose that is already stored in your blood can't be utilized. Once it consumes the glucose, the body will search for alternative fuel types and go to the fat storage for energy instead.

The fasting period shouldn't be confused with

the fasted state, as the first term means the time window during which you are not consuming any calories at all, while the second one is a phase during which the body starts to run on fats. Coincidence or not, ketosis starts at the same time as the fasted state. Ketosis is a state during which the blood sugar and insulin level are decreasing, while the ketones levels are boosting. Ketones are chemicals produced by your liver, responsible for breaking down the fat tissue. If ketones are releasing the energy from your fat tissue, by breaking it down (thus burning it), the insulin will take care of your blood sugar, so it remains regulated. Research studies have shown that ketosis (and the fasted state), start 12 hours after your last meal. If you had your last meat at 7 pm, you will enter into the ketosis state at 7 am the next day. Being in a state of ketosis is known to suppress your appetite, letting your body to focus on the fat burning process. Ketosis should not be confused with the keto-adaptation process, as they are not quite the same thing. If ketosis is a metabolic state with growing levels of ketones, the keto-adaptation process is making the body use ketones and burn the fats. Bottom line, ketosis' main goal is to train the body to run on fats, whether it's the fat reserves you have already stored or the fat you are feeding your body.

How Can You Induce It? The Main Features of a Keto Diet

So far, we established that ketosis is a part of intermittent fasting, but it can also be achieved through a different means than avoiding all food for at least 12 hours. It makes your body run on fats, but what if your body runs directly on the fats you consume and only after that on the fat reserves your body has stored? Any diet that encourages the metabolic state of ketosis is called a "keto diet." This diet is vastly different from the standard western meal plan, which is too rich in carbs, the main source of glucose. When the body runs again on glucose, the ketosis state is over, so this is something you need to avoid because fat should be the primary fuel type at all times when on keto.

You have probably heard the expression "I am cutting down on carbs" a million times. It means significantly lowering the number of carbs you consume. This is the main idea behind the keto diet, the second way to induce ketosis. That's why it is considered an LCHF (low-carb high-fat) diet. By replacing the carbs from your diet with fats, you are basically avoiding the consumption of glucose and you are making sure that your body runs on fats.

Ketosis is only a temporary phase of the intermittent fasting process, but through the keto diet, this metabolic state can be extended for a much longer period of time.

Your body is like a car, it needs fuel in order to work. What you consume will eventually be burned for energy, so why not eat more fat in order to burn fat? The body can run on the fat you feed it, but also on the fat reserves from your "tank" (fat tissue). There are several types of ketogenic diets and we will outline them all below:

- **Standard Ketogenic Diet (SKD):** is an option which involves high levels of fat consumption, moderate protein consumption, and extremely low consumption of carbs. The ratio for this diet is 75% fats, 20% proteins, and just 5% carbs. Don't be afraid of such high levels of fats, as you will set your body to burn fats, especially the ones you eat, and if you are also associating the keto diet with an intense workout, you will definitely burn fat from the fat tissues you have stored on your body.

- **Cyclical Ketogenic Diet (CKD)**: the standard keto diet can normally be used by most of the people, but for some lowering the carbs level to a minimum is too much to be done on a daily basis. This option allows you to alternate the high-carb days with the ones with lower carb intake. During a week, you can have 2 days with normal (high-carb) consumption and 5 days of the standard keto diet (carbs level at 5% each day).

- **Targeted Ketogenic Diet (TKD)**: is a plan special dedicated for bodybuilders and athletes, and which allows a higher carb intake around training times.

- **High-Protein Ketogenic Diet** represents a deviation from the standard ketogenic diet because it allows a higher protein consumption. If the standard keto diet has around 20% protein intake, this one raises to limit to 35%. Therefore, the ratio should be 60% fats, 35% proteins, and just 5% carbs.

There aren't too many people who are trying to calculate the number of carbs, proteins or fats they are consuming with each food or drink they have. Any product that comes in a box, bag, or bottle has a label with nutritional value on it. You can see plain as day the quantity for the major macronutrients and estimated calorie counts. However, we discussed so far only percentages, not exact numbers. Nutritionists agree that 5% of daily carbs should be under 50 grams, ideally under 20 grams. You are probably saying that 20 grams per day of carbs is impossible, or would be too difficult to stick to. Below you can find the food groups you can eat in order to achieve that goal. Although it may sound a bit harsh, 20 grams of carbs per day is totally doable:

- Meat. This is one of the major food types and also the best source of proteins, it can have fats (which is good), but it can also have carbs as well if the meat is more processed. Sausages and meatballs, for instance, can have a higher carb value. They have to be avoided, in order for you to stick to the 20-gram or 5%-carb limit. Also, you will need to consider what the animal ate before being slaughtered for food. If it was fed organic food and grass, that's ideal. If it was fed with concentrated food and supplements, in order to grow very quickly, that's not very good. There are plenty of proteins that can be found in meat, but the ketogenic diet is not necessarily a high-protein plan, it's more of a high-fat plan. Glucose can be created from protein, so you may need to limit the consumption of meat because it can lead to higher glucose levels, and this may knock you out of ketosis.

- Fish and seafood. This type of food is highly recommended during a keto diet, mostly because it has a bit lower protein level than red meats. Fatty fish, like salmon, are among the best choices, and tuna is also a great choice. Please avoid breaded fish, as it will turn your fish into a high-carb meal.

- Eggs can be consumed in every possible way, whether you prefer them boiled, scrambled, as omelets, or other options. Eggs are extremely keto-friendly.

- High-fat natural oils and sauces. In this category are included olive oil, garlic butter or bearnaise sauce, but also coconut oil and butter. Processed sauces (ketchup, barbeque sauces and so on) should be excluded from your diet, as these typically have lots of added sugars.

- Leafy green, fresh or frozen veggies. Make sure you include in your diet cauliflower, cabbage, broccoli, zucchini, and of course, avocado. If you consume them in a salad, make sure you pour olive oil in a consistent amount. These healthy foods can easily replace classical side dishes like rice, potatoes and even pasta.

- High-fat dairy products must be included in a keto diet. This category includes butter, high-fat cheese, and heavy cream.

- Nuts can be used as snacks during a keto diet, as they have low levels of carbs, except cashews which have more carbs than the rest of the nuts.

- Berries are usually very sweet and do contain fructose which can be converted to glucose, so they should be consumed in moderation if eaten on keto.

Now that you know what you can eat when being on this diet, we should also take a look at some of the drinks which can help you ease the keto-adaptation process.

- Water. You really can't hope for a better drink when it comes to dieting. It doesn't have any calories and it hydrates the body like no other drink on earth can. Whether you drink it still or sparkling, with ice cubes or with slices of lime or lemon, water is the best possible drink to have on keto. In fact, you will need to consume more water than when following a standard western diet, as it is critical to flush the body when doing keto.

- Coffee. This is allowed with the keto diet, but only if you drink it sugar-free. Sugar has glucose, and this will put a halt to the ketosis phase. The keto diet allows you to add a bit of cream, or butter or coconut oil for extra fat.

- Tea can be consumed at all phases of this diet, as long as there is no sugar whatsoever. You will need to avoid really sweet teas, like berry teas, because they have really high fructose levels, which can turn into sugar and knock you out of ketosis. The best options, in this case, can be black, green, herbal, mint or Orange Pekoe tea.

- Some nutritionists recommend consuming bone broth because it's very hydrating, satisfying and it also contains many nutrients and electrolytes.

Okay, so now you see what you can eat and drink during a keto diet, but what exactly you will need to avoid? The answer is pretty simple: ***CARBS!*** There are a few different categories of carbs, but by far the most important ones to take note of (and also the most harmful) are sugars and starch.

- Sugar. It's really hard to think of a more dangerous ingredient than this one. The consumption of sugar is causing some of the most serious health concerns humans are suffering from nowadays. Sugar abuse has led to more deaths than drugs, tobacco, and alcohol. All the packed products are now properly labeled informing consumers about the sugar levels of the product. Some governments have even set a tax on sugar in an effort to decrease sugar consumption among their peoples. Sugar can be found in plenty of products like breakfast cereals, donuts, ice cream, chocolate, cakes, cookies, candies, fruit juices, soft drinks, and sweets. Obviously, all of these products are strictly prohibited in this diet, and shouldn't be consumed. Artificial sweeteners are also not recommended in the keto diet, as some people's bodies react to these in the same way as they do to sugars, but a natural alternative like stevia is allowed in this meal plan.

- Starch is found in products like rice, porridge, potatoes, muesli, potato chips, French fries, pastries, pasta, and bread. There is no place for any these food types in the keto diet, as they put a stop the ketosis state due to their high carb content. Some legumes, like beans and lentils, should also be avoided because they have high levels of carbs.

- Beer is strictly forbidden by the keto diet because in most cases it has high carb levels. The carbs are easily absorbed, which is not a good thing. There are probably hundreds or thousands types of beer, some of them have been brewed to have lower carb levels, depending on the used ingredients, but overall beer is a carb nightmare for keto dieters.

- Margarine is the perfect example of how a processed product can't effectively replace a natural and organic one. It was supposed to be a good replacement option for butter, but in fact tastes worse than butter, has too many trans fats and should definitely be avoided. Nothing good can come out of margarine consumption--stick to real butter instead.

At some point, ketosis should line up with and transform into the keto-adaptation process, so ketones should work properly to extract the energy out of the fat tissue or the fat you consume. This keto-adaptation process has a few phases, which we will outline below:

1. *Carb restriction* refers to lowering the carb consumption by using a ketogenic diet to take your carb intake down to an extremely low level. You are replacing the carbs you consume with fat, making sure the body uses energy from the fat you eat, or from your fat tissue.

2. *Keto flu* marks a time frame, during which you will be exhausted and tired, due to ketones not doing their job properly. At this point, ketones are not used efficiently in extracting the energy from the fat cells. Eventually, the brain will adapt and will determine to allow the ketones to work their "magic." There is no exact science when it comes to how long the keto flu period lasts, as it depends on your sensitivity. It may take a few days or up to a few weeks, but you will eventually get over this period. One thing that can help is consuming more

water while also monitoring electrolyte intake. A dash of potassium salt and a dash of table salt on one of your meals can help keep electrolytes maintained.

3. *Familiarization with ketones.* The keto flu period is now over, as you are starting to feel better and more energized, and this is due to the keto diet. If you are activating ketosis through intermittent fasting, you should know that this way is faster, but you will need to avoid total starvation. This phase can take anywhere from two weeks to a few months.

4. *Fat burning mode.* Ketones are starting to work properly and you feel a lot more energized. This energy has to come from somewhere, and it can only come from fat tissue. This point marks the fat burning phase. During this step, you can see noticeable fat loss, better athletic performance, less hunger, better cognitive function, longer time to exhaustion and less fatigue.

5. *Keto adaptation* is when the body can run quite efficiently on body fat and the fat from your keto diet. You will no longer feel the urge to consume carbs

and get the glucose from it in order to burn it. Since the ketones are very active and effectively burning fat cells, you will experience less hunger.

6. *Metabolic flexibility.* The keto-adaptation process actually prevents addiction to the carbs, fats or ketones you use or consume. You can slightly increase the carb levels from your keto baseline of 20 carbs and still be in the ketosis metabolic state.

Benefits of Ketosis

Ketosis has many positive impacts on your body and your health, as shown by a few studies conducted so far. Carbs are the root cause for many troubles in the human body, so eliminating this cause can only lead to positive effects. Around 70% of the illnesses known today are caused by the food we eat, and carbs play a major role when it comes to the cause of these issues. Ketones are responsible for decreasing oxidative stress and inflammation, which are considered the roots of many health problems and chronic conditions.

However, the most vital benefits of ketosis are:

a) Increased control over your appetite. Plenty of people have already been in the ketosis state and they can confirm that they felt a lot less hunger. There are studies that show the loss of appetite that occurs during this state, unlike the period when the body was eating more carbs and was also craving more shortly thereafter. Carbohydrates are linked with glucose, which is the energy source they provide for the body. The keto diet eliminates carbs almost completely from your meals, preventing the consumption of glucose and thus, preventing the increase of blood sugar and insulin levels.

b) Potential weight loss. Proteins and fats are the most useful macronutrients. In order to activate ketosis and to make the body use the energy from fat cells, you will have to eat mostly fat and a minimal daily dosage of carbs. Ketones will extract the energy from your fat tissue so the body will run on the fat stored or freshly eaten. Since ketosis suppresses your appetite, you will no longer feel the need to eat carbohydrates (so no glucose for you), and this leads to regulating the insulin level which, in turn, regulates the blood sugar levels. In the meantime, the amount of ketones is growing rapidly, so they should easily work on reserved fats, increasing the fat burning process and resulting in substantial weight loss.

c) Prediabetes and diabetes reversal. During ketosis, insulin is set free to regulate the blood sugar, thus lowering it to a decent level. For people suffering from such health problems, this can mean no more need for diabetes medication.

d) Improved athletic performance. Just think about it! The fat burning process can transform the fat into muscles. Less fat and more muscles lead to a stronger, faster and more agile body, thus resulting in better athletic performance.

e) Epilepsy control. The keto diet has proven to be efficient when it comes to controlling epilepsy in both adults and children who previously had not responded to anti-seizure medication.

The keto diet is an example of nutrient-deprivation program that has extremely positive impacts on your body and health, as you can see above. However, you need to know that not everything is amazing with this diet, as it has some downsides. Minimizing the carb intake is without any doubt a positive thing, as we can live just fine without many carbs at all. Your body will experience different feelings when being on this diet, and some of them may not be very pleasant. Probably the main side effect of the keto diet is the keto flu period, as described above as a phase of the keto-adaptation process. Unfortunately, it's not something that you can necessarily avoid, but it does depend on each individual's response to induction on the diet. During this period, you may need to consider less exercising, eating more fats and increasing your water and salt consumption to bring about the right balance as your body grows accustomed to keto.

Everyone can agree that ketosis has an impact on boosting the fat burning process, but what about muscle mass? Is protein deprivation going to generate muscle loss? Nutritionists say that the body mass needs a certain protein intake in order to be maintained. Depriving yourself of this quantity of proteins can have damaging effects on your muscle tissue, but it doesn't *have* to.

As you already know, ketosis can be induced through intermittent fasting as well. Studies have shown that the growth hormone level increases through the fasting process. If you work out during this phase, you will most likely be able to preserve your muscle mass. It's the same thing with the keto diet: a workout can save your muscle mass, regardless of how many proteins you eat. Remember, ketosis is about metabolic flexibility so you can play with the protein levels in your diet once in a while and find out the right levels for your body's needs. In other words, you can alternate the standard ketogenic diet with the high-protein ketogenic diet, to make sure you have the necessary proteins in you to prevent muscle loss. Other disadvantages of ketosis may include constipation, vitamin deficiency, and kidney damage.

The Benefits of a Ketogenic Diet

Wait, so we can eat fatty foods now?

Many of you may be confused by all these sudden changes in dietary opinions. I don't blame you. Not too long ago, it was considered bad to consume foods that were high in fat because people believed that it was the fat in the foods that were making *us* fat.

I mean, it's not a horrible assumption to make. However, this theory has been blown right out of the water and now everyone and their grandmothers are talking about the benefits of a high-fat diet. That's probably why you're here, reading this book, right?

You've heard about this diet from someone else and they can't stop talking about how much weight they've lost. However, you're skeptical and I would be too. So, here are some answers to a few questions you might be asking right now.

What is a Ketogenic Diet?

The ketogenic diet, along with a few other high-fat diets, has gained popularity over the past few decades and is taking the unhealthy world by storm. It's no wonder everyone is talking about it because, if done right, the diet really does work for causing effective weight loss and health management. There's a simple science behind it but I know you're not here to read a bunch of blabber about science so I'll make it quick.

The basic way to understand the ketogenic diet is it is a way to reprogram your body to burn fat for energy instead of using carbohydrates. The easiest way to do this is to change your diet in a way where you eat more fat and fewer carbs.

Our bodies have a preferred source of energy. Yes, our bodies are really that picky. They prefer to take the glucose in our bodies and convert that into energy for the brain and other functions. The glucose in our bodies that is used for energy mostly comes from carbohydrates. The problem with this is that we generally tend to eat more carbohydrates, foods that are high in starch and sugar, than our body can actually use for energy, and that's where a lot of carb-related health problems come from.

The main process that our bodies go through with the standard western diet is to eat carbs like they're going out of fashion, and then our bodies burn a small amount of the carbs for energy. The carbs that aren't burned, though, become stored sugar for the body to burn for energy later. However, we eat more carbs and the body turns some of that into energy instead of taking from the stored sugar and again it doesn't use all of the carbs so more sugar gets stored. This process keeps repeating and it leaves us with an abundance of stored sugar that our body is never going to get a chance to use.

During a ketogenic diet, you eat more fats and fewer carbohydrates. This starves the body of carbs which leads to the body utilizing a clever backup system we have. When the body doesn't have enough glucose, which comes from carbs, the liver is designed to instead turn stored fat into energy for the brain and other bodily functions.

The liver takes stored fat and the fat that you eat and it breaks it down into ketones and fatty acids. When you're the body has a lot of ketones in it, you're in a state known as ketosis.

Ketosis and Ketones:

Once the body realizes that there isn't any more glucose or stored sugar for it to turn into the energy, it goes to plan B. The liver takes the stored fat in the body and breaks it down into fatty acids and ketones. These ketones are the most important part of this because they allow the body to break down stored fat, and that is what the body decides to use to get energy instead of glucose. Ketones help to replace the body's natural source for energy and it actually provides a better form of energy than glucose.

When your body has a certain amount of ketones in it you are sent into a state known as ketosis. This state is the entire reason people decide to start a ketogenic diet in the first place. Ketosis is where your body is completely free of any stored sugar or glucose of any kind and the body is running on stored fat. The only source of energy your body has is the fat that you're eating and the fat on your body.

When your body has no choice but to turn the stuff you're eating into energy, that's when you start losing weight. Because what you're eating is being broken down and turned into energy, nothing gets stored and you don't gain any weight. Just remember that you won't gain weight but you won't lose it either unless you do something extra, like exercise or keeping an eye on calorie intake.

Long story short, a ketogenic diet works!

Yes, it does, and there's also a lot more to gain other than maintaining or losing weight. It's true that most people choose a ketogenic diet because they want to find an effective means of weight control, but there are many other health benefits that come along with taking on this diet.

The Physical Benefits of a Ketogenic Diet

The ketogenic diet has only recently been made popular amongst those eager to lose weight. However, it has been used for plenty of other reasons in the medical field for quite some time now, and research has shown that this meal plan can have a variety of medical benefits, beyond improving your metabolism.

The positive impact on diabetes and prediabetes

When speaking about prediabetes and diabetes, you need to understand terms like *high blood sugar* and *insulin level*. As your body is mainly used to running on glucose, and so far you fed your body through a diet rich in carbs, the glucose you consume will not entirely be used for energy. *Burning* glucose is what energizes the body, not *eating* it.

Due to high carb intake and also a very sedentary lifestyle, this glucose is not burned entirely. Therefore, the body becomes lazy at burning fats, and that's why you don't have the energy to do many things. You have to understand that your body is like a power plant, it needs fuel in the form of glucose, but it has to generate energy. That's why you mostly feel tired even when you are not doing anything. The processed food of today is more calorie dense than nutrient dense because it has all the calories, but none of the nutrients required for the proper functioning of the body.

When you eat food with a high concentration of glucose, it will not be consumed entirely, so the remaining glucose gets stored to your blood. This increases your blood sugar and insulin level. Insulin is the main anabolic hormone of your body and it's released by the pancreas. It should play a major role in regulating the blood sugar, but when you constantly feed your body with high levels of glucose, it simply can't handle that kind of glucose overload. This is when your body is in an insulin resistant state. At this point, when insulin doesn't work properly to lower the blood sugar, you can be entering a prediabetes phase. By continuing on the same path you will almost certainly end up with diabetes.

The keto diet eliminates the cause of this condition and by eradicating the thing that prevents the insulin hormone to work as it should. It's a carb-deprivation diet designed to lower the glucose level to the point where it can be completely burned and consumed. Replacing the carbs with fats can set the body to run on a different type of fuel. The body runs on what you are feeding it, and this ketogenic eating habit has been proven to improve the functionality of the insulin. Your body can't burn the glucose stored in your blood, but when the insulin senses that there is no more glucose coming, it gets activated and starts to do its job. Minimizing the amount of glucose you consume will force the body to almost immediately burn the glucose you just ate and begin its search for an alternative fuel type.

The body can quickly adapt in this scenario, that's why it starts to produce ketone bodies, which are the required tools to break through fat and release its stored energy. If ketones take care of fat, insulin gets reactivated in the meantime, and lowers the blood sugar, regulating it to a normal level. There are specific studies that showed an increased insulin sensitivity of 75%. Also, a different study conducted on persons with type 2 diabetes discovered that 7 of the 21 subjects stopped using diabetes medication after the keto diet was introduced.

As you are already aware, the keto diet favors weight loss, and excessive weight is a common thing among people suffering from type 2 diabetes or who are in a prediabetic state. Another study has shown that the keto group lost 24.4 pounds, compared to 15.2 pounds of the non-keto group. Weight loss is very important for type 2 diabetes subjects. More than 95% of the subjects in the keto group managed to cut down on diabetes medication after this diet, compared to 62% of the non-keto group. These findings show how the keto diet can prevent or reverse the prediabetes and diabetes phase.

But that's not all. The ketogenic diet has plenty of other benefits when it comes to medical conditions or diseases:

- Heart disease. Obviously, the keto diet

leads directly to less body fat, and indirectly to lower cholesterol level, blood sugar, and blood pressure. By having these effects, the keto diet has a positive impact on preventing heart disease.

- Cancer. The keto diet can slow tumor growth with several types of cancer (during the incipient phase, of course). In many cases, cancer can be caused by the food or drink we consume.

- Alzheimer's and Parkinson's disease. The ketogenic diet is known to improve mental and cognitive function, thus preventing or slowing the progression of neurodegenerative diseases like Parkinson's and Alzheimer's.

- Epilepsy. There are studies showing positive impacts of the ketogenic diet in reducing seizures in epileptic children as well as adults.

- Polycystic ovarian syndrome. High insulin levels may be one of the causes of polycystic ovarian syndrome. The keto diet reduces the insulin level, thus lowering the chances of this syndrome.

- Brain injuries. A study conducted on animals showed that this diet is able to reduce the effects of concussions and the aid in reducing recovery time after a brain injury.

- Acne. Excessive glucose consumed and in your blood can be a cause of acne. The keto diet lowers the insulin level and blood sugar so it may help improve acne or other skin conditions.

The Benefits of Keto Snacks for your Ketogenic Diet

When you are thinking of snacks, thoughts of sugar, salt and probably plenty of chemicals we can't even pronounce come to mind, which is not quite healthy for your body. Such food types don't have much nutrient value, and some of them are simply calorie bombs. These snacks are designed to fill your body with glucose, which will eventually get stored in your blood. They are calorie dense, but they are not nutrient dense, so hunger pangs and cravings return with a vengeance a short time after consuming them, leading to a cycle of bad eating habits.

However, with the ketogenic diet, snacks play a different role, as not only they are permitted, but they are also highly recommended. Standard snacks are carb bombs; however, keto snacks are the exact opposite, as they focus more on the fats and have a minimal (or nil) carb level. Without a doubt, the keto snacks are designated fat bombs to serve the ultimate purpose of the ketogenic diet, which is to make sure the body uses fat as an energy source.

You can compare your body to a typical car. It uses fuel to burn energy and to function properly. In this case, fat is the cleaner type of fuel, which preserves and enhances the function of your body. Unlikely other diets, the keto diet doesn't necessarily mean calorie restriction, but it does mean changing the food you eat, including the snacks you consume. Most diets wouldn't allow snacks, but this one encourages them. So if you are a snack enthusiast, and snacks are something you simply can't renounce, then the keto diet is the one for you. Besides the obvious benefits of these keto foods (health and physical benefits), eating keto snacks can have impressive effects from a psychological point of view, as well, because you feel better about yourself when you can eat snacks and actually lose weight. When you enjoy what you eat and you also get solid results, there shouldn't be any reason you can't keep the diet ongoing. Keto snacks are the special spice which makes this diet so popular, and are the reason people worldwide are using this diet over the long term.

Keto Grocery List

When deciding to take on the keto diet, you will definitely need to clean out your refrigerator and get rid of most of the processed foods you have in the pantry. Keto is not only about maximizing the fat level you consume, but also about eating more organic, more natural foods. This radical change in your diet needs to start first in your refrigerator, as you have to completely change what you store in there. That's why you need to ask yourself how processed the food you are eating is. If you see beef with just salt or pepper, that's completely fine, but if you have beef with soy, hydrolyzed corn protein, fructose and so on, that's something you need to get rid of. As mentioned in the previous chapter, the ketogenic diet encourages the consumption of snacks, but the snacks allowed are the exact opposite of the ones you are probably used to. Below you can find a shopping list with plenty of stuff you will want to buy to enjoy keto snacks:

- Almonds
- Almond butter
- Beef jerky
- Beef sticks (check those carb counts!)
- Blackberries

- Brazil nuts
- Cheese chips;
- Cheese slices
- Cheese wedges
- Cocoa nibs
- Coconut oil
- Cottage cheese
- Dark chocolate
- Deli meat
- Flaxseed crackers
- Greek yogurt
- Sugar-free Jell-O
- Kale chips
- Macadamia nuts
- Macadamia nut butter
- Meat bar
- Olives
- Peanut butter

- Pecans
- Pepperoni slices
- Pickles
- Pork rinds
- Protein bars (carefully scrutinize carb counts)
- Pumpkin seeds
- Sardines
- Seaweed snacks
- Smoked oysters
- Sunflower seeds
- String cheese
- Toasted coconut flakes
- Walnuts
- Avocado
- Cauliflower
- Broccoli
- Eggs

- Mushrooms

- Guacamole (be cautious about carb counts--you can use avocado to make your own)

- Peppers (check those carbs first)

- And more!

As you can see, the list is quite long, and some of the ingredients may be refrigerated and stored for a longer period of time, while others are more perishable, so you need to consume them fresh buy them more often.

Low Carb Keto Snack Recipes

Let's Cook!

Avocados are the Devil's Eggs:

The deviled egg is a dish normally frowned upon by diet enthusiasts. This is because it usually contains a high amount of commercial mayonnaise. The high amount of mayonnaise in a normal deviled egg is enough to ruin any diet, but this is not your average deviled egg recipe.

This recipe doesn't contain mayonnaise at all but replaces it with something just as tasty; avocados. Remember that although this is low in carbs and high in fat it does still contain *some* carbs. The more of it you eat the further away you get from the keto diet, so eat in moderation.

Recommended serving: 1 egg

Ingredients:

- 2 hard boiled eggs
- 1 ripe avocado
- Keto-friendly seasoning (optional)

Method:

Place a pot on the high heat with just enough water in it to cover the eggs. Place the lid on and let the eggs boil for 2 minutes.

Meanwhile, you can halve the avocado, scoop the insides out, and place it in a medium-sized bowl.

After the eggs have been boiling for 2 minutes, remove them from the heat and put them under running cold water to stop the cooking. Leave them in cold water to cool.

When the eggs are cool, you can peel the shell off carefully. Once the shells are off, carefully half the two eggs and scoop the cooked yolks out.

Place the yolks in the bowl with the avocado and mix well until the mixture is smooth and creamy.

You can now fill the halved eggs with as much of the mixture you want.

Season with keto-friendly spices. I recommend chili powder to add a nice kick to the taste. (Optional)

Depending on the size of the eggs and the size of the avocado you have, the number of ingredients may need to be adjusted.

You can make this recipe in larger batches and put the rest in the fridge for snacking in the future.

Stuffed Mushrooms:

Mushrooms make a tasty holder for other tasty treats. Mushrooms are low carb and anti-inflammatory snack. It's the perfect addition to any low carb diet. Small mushrooms are the best because they help you eat less, which is always good when on a diet, even this one.

You can stuff these mushrooms with whatever you like--as long as it's low-carb--but here are a few examples to get you started.

Cheesy Mushrooms

Recommended Serving: 2 mushroom cups

Ingredients:

- A pack of small mushrooms

- ½ cup of grated cheese
- Keto-friendly seasoning (optional)
- Coconut oil

Method:

Take the pack of small mushrooms and hollow them out. You can do this by carefully cutting out the stem so the mushroom forms a cup. You can keep the stems and use them in another dish if you don't want them to go to waste.

Place a pan on the stove on a low heat and place a small drop of coconut oil on the bottom of the pan. Use a paper towel to spread the coconut oil around the pan.

Place the mushrooms in the pan and cook them slowly.

Season the mushrooms with Keto friendly seasoning. For this recipe, I recommend a pinch of sea salt. (Optional)

Remove the mushrooms from the heat when they are cooked.

Take an oven-safe dish and cover the bottom with a non-stick sheet.

Use a spoon to scoop the mushrooms from the

pan to the oven safe dish. Line them up to they aren't close to each other.

Stuff each mushroom with a bit of the grated cheese. The mushrooms will be warm, so it's okay if the cheese starts to melt.

When all the mushrooms are stuffed with a bit of cheese, set the oven to grill and slide the mushrooms in.

Don't close the oven door. Wait until the cheese all melted and the top is slightly brown before removing them from the oven.

You don't want the cheese to be too brown or else it will become crunchy. You just want the top to be a little crisp while the inside is soft and juicy.

This recipe doesn't call for a specific type of cheese so you can pick and choose what you like. Keep in mind how keto-friendly the cheese is before you use it.

You can make this recipc in large batches and keep in the fridge. If you're feeling like a snack just pop them in the microwave and eat up.

Avocado Mushrooms

Recommended Serving: 2 mushroom cups

Ingredients:

- A pack of small mushrooms
- One ripe avocado
- Coconut oil
- Keto friendly seasoning (optional)

Method:

Hollow out the mushrooms by cutting the stem out carefully. You can save the stems and use them in another dish.

Put a drop of coconut oil into the pan and use a paper towel to spread the oil along the bottom of the pan.

Put the mushrooms in the pan and cook them on low heat.

Meanwhile, halve the avocado and scoop the insides into a medium-sized bowl.

You can season both the mushrooms and the avocado is you wish. Remember that the more you season, the more calories you add, and some seasonings (like garlic powder or granulated onion) are higher in carbs than others. I recommended a pinch of sea salt on the mushrooms and mix a pinch of cumin into the avocado. (Optional)

When the mushrooms are cooked, you can remove them from the pan and put them on a plate.

Spoon the avocado into the mushrooms. Put just enough avocado in to fill the mushroom cups but not so it overflows.

The mushrooms are now ready to eat. If you want to grill the top in the oven to add a bit of a crunch, you can, but they taste perfectly fine just as they are.

The avocado doesn't do so well if you reheat it so I don't suggest making this snack in a large batch. Make enough to eat in a day but don't save leftovers in the fridge for later as it won't taste or look as great.

Bacon and Mushroom Bites

Recommended Serving: 3 mushroom cups

Ingredients:

- A pack of small mushrooms

- Bacon (diced to small bits)
- Coconut oil
- Keto friendly seasoning (optional)

Method:

Hollow out the mushrooms by carefully cutting out the stems. You can save the stems for later use, if desired.

Put a small drop of coconut oil into a pan and use a paper towel to spread it over the bottom of the pan.

Put the mushrooms in the pan and cook on low heat.

Chop and dice some bacon into small bits.

Put some coconut oil into a second pan and let the oil heat up on the stove. When the heat has thinned out the oil you can move the pan around so the oil can spread across the bottom of the pan.

Now add the bacon to the second pan and cook it on medium heat. Watch out because the oil might splatter as you add the bacon.

You can season both the bacon and the mushrooms, but the more seasoning you add the more calories you're be eating. I recommended a pinch of sea salt the mushrooms, but the bacon is likely salty enough by itself. (Optional)

When the mushrooms are cooked you can spoon them on to a plate. When the bacon is cooked you can start stuffing the mushroom caps.

Depending on the size of the mushrooms, ½ a teaspoon of bacon should be enough for each cap.

This is a great recipe to make in large batches and put some in the fridge for later. If you watch the calorie count carefully, you can add a bit of cheese on top of the bacon and throw it in the oven on grill/broil.

Fried Mushrooms

Simply frying mushrooms in coconut oil and sprinkling on a pinch of sea salt makes for a great snack. So fry some up, sit back with a bowl and fork, and enjoy the simple, natural taste of the mushrooms. I recommend using the freshest, highest quality mushrooms for this so you can enjoy their flavor more fully.

Recommended serving: 5 small mushrooms

Kale Chips:

This is a snack that you can buy already premade, but it's also quite easy to make yourself and this way, you'll know exactly what ingredients went into your snack. Kale is a great-tasting, fresh ingredient to add to any dish. So stock that fridge with kale and let's get cooking.

Recommended Serving: ½ a bunch of kale

Ingredients:

- 1 bunch of fresh kale
- Olive oil
- Keto-friendly seasoning (optional)

Method:

Preheat the oven to a medium heat setting.

Take the bunch of kale and rinse thoroughly underneath a cold water tap.

Separate the stems from each other and place them on a dish towel to dry during preparation.

Take a baking tray and lay a sheet of non-stick paper along the bottom of it.

Rip the kale leaves off of the stem one by one and place them on the baking tray. It's okay if they're still a bit wet. Make sure you keep the leaves you break off large because they will shrink considerably while baking, and don't worry about keeping them separate.

Once you have all the kale on the baking tray drizzle a small amount of olive oil over it, about 1 teaspoon. Use your hands to toss the kale around so the olive oil is distributed evenly over all of the kale.

You can sprinkle some keto-friendly seasoning on the kale and toss it again to distribute the seasoning evenly. I recommend some sea salt, but it's up to you in the end. (Optional)

Now you can place the baking tray into an oven on medium heat.

It should take about 10 minutes for the kale to bake to a crisp. It may take longer depending on how wet the kale was when you were preparing it. Watch it closely and every now and again open the oven and use a wooden spoon to stir the kale around a little bit.

You want the kale to be crispy but you want to take it out before it starts browning.

Once the kale chips are baked, you can take them out of the oven and toss them into a bowl for a quick and healthy snack. You can also enjoy the kale chips with a cheesy or creamy keto-friendly dip.

I don't recommend making this snack in a large batch or keeping them for too long. Make enough to eat in a day and put the rest of the unbaked kale into the fridge for use in salads or to use for more kale chips a different day.

Zucchini Chips:

Another great alternative for healthy chips is zucchini chips. Although they aren't as quick to make as kale chips, they are just as easy and taste amazing. So if you have enough patience to bake them then give them a try.

Recommended Serving: 1 large zucchini

Ingredients:

- 1 large zucchini

- Olive oil (optional)

- Keto-friendly seasoning (optional)

Method:

Preheat the oven to medium heat.

Slice the zucchini into thin round slices. The thinner you can slice them the quicker they'll bake and the crispier they'll be. Try making sure they're all around the same thickness so they bake evenly.

Take a baking tray, and cover the bottom of the tray with a sheet of non-stick paper. Alternatively, you could use cooking spray to stop the zucchini from sticking.

Place the sliced zucchini on the baking tray. Arrange it so the zucchini are sitting next to each other. They can be touching each other but none of them can be on top of another or they will not bake evenly.

You can drizzle a small amount of olive oil onto the zucchini for a bit of flavor. You can also sprinkle some keto friendly seasoning on to the zucchini. I recommend some sea salt. (Optional)

Place in the oven and bake on medium heat for about 1 hour then turn the zucchinis over and bake on the other side for about 1 hour.

You want the zucchini to be dried, crispy, and golden brown or just slightly brown.

Let the zucchini chips cool before eating them. You can serve them by themselves or with a creamy, keto-friendly dip. These chips take a long time to prepare but they are worth it.

You can make these in a large batch if you don't mind them being cold when you eat them. Warming them up could take away from their crispy texture.

Cheesy Broccoli:

I know what you're going to say and yes I know broccoli is not the most beloved food. But how can you say no when it's covered in cheese? I know that I can never say no to a bit of cheese.

Recommended Serving: 6 ounces of broccoli

Ingredients:

- 6 ounces of broccoli, fresh or frozen
- 1 cup of grated cheese

- 1 tablespoon of butter (optional)
- Keto-friendly seasoning (optional)

Method:

Preheat the oven to high heat.

If frozen; let the broccoli defrost and then place in a pot with water. Place the pot on a high heat and let that boil for a few minutes.

If fresh; separate the broccoli into florets and then place in a pot with water. Place the pot on a high heat and let that boil for a few minutes.

You can season the water with sea salt before placing the broccoli in to boil. (Optional)

You want to let the broccoli boil until it is cooked but it should retain its fresh green color and its soft, chewy texture.

Take a baking tray and cover the bottom of it with a non-stick sheet of paper or some cooking spray.

Drain the water from the broccoli and place the broccoli onto the baking tray. Make sure the broccoli florets are separated from one another.

You can add some butter to the tray, putting a small bit on each piece of broccoli, and you can add some keto-friendly seasoning. (Optional)

Sprinkle a bit of the grated cheese over each piece of broccoli. Make sure the cheese is covering the head of the broccoli floret so it can "soak in."

Then pop the tray into the oven and bake for about 20 minutes or until the cheese starts to brown.

Wait to cool down slightly before serving.

This is a dish you can make in large batches and keep in the fridge for later. It makes a great snack and it works well as a side for a main dish too.

Cream Cheese Choco Fudge

This kind of snack is considered a sweet fat bomb and it shouldn't be too complicated to prepare. You will need for it different kinds of ingredients like vanilla extract (one teaspoon), 1 cup of softened cream cheese, ⅓ cup of unsweetened cocoa powder, 1 teaspoon of Stevia, 1 cup of butter, 1 ounce of unsweetened baking chocolate, unsweetened almond butter (1 cup), and regular butter (1 cup).

Please follow the instructions below in order to prepare this delicious snack:

1. Put parchment paper onto a baking tray.

2. Melt the butter and the baking chocolate in a pan, at medium heat. At this point you can add the almond butter and blend it in the pan.

3. This is the time to add the cream cheese, then you will need to blend more.

4. Turn off the heat and add the dry ingredients. You will need to blend it until you get a nice creamy and smooth mixture.

5. You will need to pour the mixture into the baking tray and make sure it spreads evenly. Put the mixture in your refrigerator.

The whole tray should yield around 16 servings. The mixture has 26 grams of fat, and just 5 grams of carbs, 3 grams of proteins, 2.5 grams of fiber and 1 gram of sugar.

Raspberry Heaven

Fat and sweet should be two of the main characteristics of these kinds of snacks. Raspberry Heaven seems to be the ideal dessert in this case, as it's very sweet without being too sugary, full of fat, but extremely low on carbs. For this kind of snack, you will need coconut flour (a quarter of a cup), almond flour (half cup), 1 teaspoon of vanilla, Swerve sweetener (2 tablespoons), full-fat cream cheese (8.8 ounces) and frozen raspberries (1 cup). For coating, you will need extra virgin coconut oil (1.4 ounces) and 2.8 ounces of dark chocolate. It already sounds delicious, but wait until you find out how easily this miracle dessert is prepared. Here are the instructions:

1. In a food processor, you will need to blend and mix together the frozen raspberries, Swerve, and cream cheese.

2. You can add now both types of flour (coconut and almond) and mix again.

3. Take the mixture out and place it in a special ball-shaped lollipop tray. If you don't have such a tray, you can shape the mixtures into balls using your own hands.

4. Freeze it for about 50 minutes.

5. While the balls are freezing, you can prepare your coating. You will need to use a glass bowl in order to melt the chocolate and pour the coconut oil. The

glass bowl can be placed over a saucepan which has some water in it (about a cup) and put it on the stove at high heat. Turn off the heat when the chocolate is melted (make sure you don't burn it) and allow it to cool slightly.

6. Take the mixture from your freezer and use a wooden stick or small silicone spatula to coat the frozen ball with chocolate. Dip the balls in the mixture, until the chocolate hardens and all balls have been dipped.

7. Put each ball in a tray which has greaseproof paper. Place them in the refrigerator for about 20 minutes.

This dessert should yield you 16 servings, it has 136 calories, 13 grams of regular fat, 7 grams of saturated fat, 3 grams of protein and only 2 grams of carbs. You can actually get addicted to them, they are that delicious!

Crumbs N' Cream Bombs

If you are looking for something a little more consistent, but still incredibly high in fats and very low on carbs, then perhaps the right option for you is crumbs n' cream bombs. This sweet treat yields 6 servings and is a bit more complex when it comes to the ingredients and also when it comes to cooking it, but the effort is worth it.

For the crumbs, you will need 2 tablespoons of coconut oil, a pinch kosher salt, almond flour (half a cup), 2 tablespoons of Swerve, half a teaspoon of instant coffee and 3 teaspoons of unsweetened cocoa powder.

For your cream you will need vanilla extract (2 teaspoons), heavy whipping cream (half of cup), another pinch kosher salt, coconut milk (half a cup) and erythritol or other sugar-free powdered sweetener (2 tablespoons). You might already think already that this snack is too demanding, however, if you follow the instructions below, you should be able to prepare this delicious snack with ease.

1. You will need to make the crumbs first. Put the almond flour in a pan over medium heat and toast it lightly until it turns a golden color. The whole process shouldn't take longer than 4 minutes.

2. Take the golden almond flour and place it in a small bowl, in which you can also put the coffee, cocoa, salt, and Swerve. Stir them thoroughly and then add the coconut oil, and continue to mix until you get a smooth mixture.

3. This recipe calls for 6 cupcake liners. Press the crumb mixture (⅓ of it) into each cupcake liner evenly. Each cupcake will have around one third from this crumb mixture to be used as "base". Put them in your freezer.

4. In order to prepare the cream, you will need to melt the sweetener, coconut milk and salt at medium heat. Mix until you have a smooth texture going and then pour the mixture into a bowl and let it cool in the freezer for a while.

5. In the meantime, you will need to whisk up the whipping cream until it gets fluffy, then add vanilla and the mixture from the previous step and then you will need to stir.

6. Now is the time to add the remaining two-thirds of "crumbs" from the first steps and fold it into the mixture;

7. The mixture has to be poured on top of the crumb bases, which should be frozen solid by now, after being left in the freezer. Freeze the whole thing until it's solid enough to be served.

This snack has 230 calories and 24 grams of fat (14 grams of saturated fat), 4 grams of carbs, 3 grams of protein.

Chocolate Peppermint Bombs

A very refreshing option when it comes to keto snacks are chocolate peppermint bombs which are very delicious and can be downright addictive. This dessert recipe creates 19 servings and it's another sweet treat that involves a n filling and a coating.

For the filling, you will need 1 teaspoon of peppermint extract, 12 drops of Stevia, coconut butter (½ cup) and also coconut oil (½ cup).

For the coating, you will need vanilla extract (about 1 teaspoon), Stevia (20 drops), half of cup of cocoa powder and coconut oil (½ cup). As you can see below, preparing this dessert is about as uncomplicated as it gets.

1. First, you will need to melt in a saucepan at medium heat the coconut butter and oil.

2. Pour it into a mixing bowl and then add peppermint extract and Stevia. You will need to blend these very well.

3. Put the mixture into an ice cube tray or cupcake liners. You will need 2 tablespoons for each mold. Then place everything into the freezer for 1 hour;

4. While the filling is freezing, you will need to prepare the coating. Put all the ingredients into a bowl together and mix, but make sure you melt the coconut oil first.

5. Take the filling mixture out of the mold and just dip every one of them in the coating mixture.

6. Put everything to freeze and serve when the coating is solid.

This snack has only 130 calories and it consists of 13 grams of fat (10 grams of saturated fat), 2 grams of carbs and 1 gram of fiber.

Pumpkin Pie Fat Bombs

When it comes to sweet-tasting to fat-bomb snacks, you really can't have a keto diet without this one, the pumpkin pie fat bomb. This dessert should yield 12 servings and is a favorite of keto dieters across the world.

For this snack, you will need a pinch of ground clove, vanilla extract (¼ teaspoon), ground ginger (1 teaspoon), pumpkin puree (¾ cup), ground cinnamon (1 tablespoon), Himalayan salt (a quarter of a teaspoon), half a cup of unsweetened shredded coconut, half a cup of coconut oil, collagen (¼ cup) and 20 drops of Stevia. This is a long list of ingredients, but using the simple instructions below you should be able to whip up a delicious dessert.

1. Line baking sheet with 12 mini muffin silicone molds.

2. In a blender, mix together the coconut oil, Stevia, shredded coconut, and salt until smooth and drippy.

3. Remove a quarter cup of the above mixture, then add the remaining ingredients and blend again.

4. Pour this mixture evenly into the 12 molds. Press the mixture firmly into the mold.

5. Now, with the remaining quarter cup from step 3, pour this over the top of each fat bomb. This will create a layered effect.

6. Place on the baking sheet then leave in the freezer for 1 hour, then serve.

Calories: 202 Carbs: 2g Fat: 21g Protein: 3.5g Fiber: 3.4g[1]

Ferrero Rocher Fat Bombs

What??? Homemade Ferrero Rocher, is it even possible? It looks like the keto diet not only is very permissive when it comes to snacks, but it also encourages you to try your favorite ones in a new way.

The ingredient list includes vanilla extract (half a teaspoon), ground hazelnuts (¾ cup), coconut oil (3 tablespoons), Erythritol (2 tablespoons) 1 ounce of dark chocolate (which has about 85% cocoa), baking cocoa powder (half a tablespoon), chopped and whole hazelnuts and nuts (half a cup). This is a must-try for anyone who felt that giving up Ferrero Rocher was the most difficult part of going keto. Here is how you can sate that craving for that sweet treat without having to go out of keto to do it:

1. You can use a saucepan or the microwave oven to melt the dark

---

[1] O'Neill, M. (2018). *Keto Fat Bombs Cookbook The #1 Low Carb & High Fat Snacks Cookbook for Ketogenic Diets, Lazy People & Weight Loss (5 Minute Fat Burning Keto Fat Bomb Recipes)*. Christopher Raymont, p.66.

chocolate and the coconut oil. Make sure they are fully melted.

2. Then you will need to put the following ingredients into a blender or a food processor: the vanilla extract, cocoa powder, hazelnuts, and Erythritol. Blend them all together. You can then add the mixture from the first step into the food processor and blend again.

3. Put the whole thing into the freezer for about 10 minutes, and then make the Ferrero Rocher copycat balls using your hands to roll the mixture around the hazelnuts so you will have right in the middle.

4. Once you have 10 balls, you can roll each ball into the chopped nuts and hazelnut, until these balls are fully covered. Now you have 10 Ferrero Rocher balls, using a keto-friendly recipe, but it's at least as delicious as the original. This dessert is ready to be served right away.

This dessert has 145 carbs, but also 14 grams of fat (2.4 grams of saturated fat), 1.7 grams of fiber and 1.9 grams of protein.

Blueberry Fat Bombs

One of the best desserts you can try during the keto diet is the blueberry fat bomb, as it has plenty of fats and is low enough in carbs to be considered keto.

You can play with the recipe and add different types of berries, however, the basic list of ingredients should include: liquid stevia (8 drops), melted coconut oil (half a cup), melted coconut butter (half a cup), 2 ½ ounces of softened cream cheese, unsweetened coconut cream (¼ cup), ¾ cup of divided blueberries. In order to prepare the dessert, you will need to follow the instructions below:

1. Put half a cup of berries, cream cheese, and coconut cream into a food processor. Blend them all together until it takes the form of a smooth mixture. Add in the stevia, coconut oil and coconut butter, and then blend again.

2. "Fill up each well of a 12-cup silicone mold or mini muffin tin lined with cupcake wrappers with an equal amount of the blueberry mixture and drop the remaining blueberries on top.

3. Place in the freezer until hardened, about 30 minutes. Store in the refrigerator.

Silicone molds are extremely helpful when you're on a ketogenic diet, especially if you're planning to make fat bombs a regular part of your diet. If you don't want to purchase silicone molds, you can use ice cube trays, but it will be harder to remove the bombs from the trays."[2]

Zero Carb Keto Snacks

In plenty of situations the difference between no carbs and carbs in a meal can be made by the sauce you added to the meal. Since carbs are messing up our health and our physical well-being, there is no wonder that plenty of people have tried to cut down on carbs or to eliminate them from their diets completely. The keto diet follows the basic principle of LCHF (low-carb,

---

[2] Boyers, L. (n.d.). *Keto Snacks From Sweet and Savory Fat Bombs to Pizza Bites and Jalapeno Poppers, 100 Low-Carb Snacks for Every Craving.* New York: Adams Media, p.156

high-fat), but did you know that you can even enjoy zero-carb foods while on the keto diet? That's right--there are keto snacks that don't have *any* carbs at all, and can basically be eaten freely until you reach a state of satiety. These snacks can guarantee ketosis and aid your body in becoming keto adapted so that it will produce and use ketones to extract the energy it needs from existing fat tissue. Also, the food that you will be eating only have fats and proteins, so if you are a bodybuilder, you may want to pay close attention to the following zero-carb keto snacks.

The food types which have or can have 0 carbs are:

- Beef jerky - depending on the flavorings you use for this meat, you can actually have 0 carbs with it. Sauces and spices can add a few carbs in there. However, you will need to be careful with this meal, as it has high protein levels so you will need to consume it moderately.

- Pork rinds - just like with beef jerky, additional sauces or spices can raise the carb count, but this meal is extremely popular and comes highly recommended for a keto diet, as it has higher levels of fat and appropriate levels of protein.

- Celery sticks - should be consumed in moderate amounts, although they have few carbs.

- Lettuce is one of the vegetables with close to 0 carb levels. You can pair it with meat or other veggies, for healthy and yummy ketogenic snacks and light lunches.

- Shirataki noodles - not only they have close to 0 carbs, they also have almost 0 calories, as well. A great replacement for lo mein, yakisoba, or even Italian-style pasta dishes.

- Chicken strips in coconut oil - chicken is known to have zero carbs if you are not adding any sauces to it, but always avoid breading chicken or you will get knocked out of ketosis. Frying the chicken in coconut oil will not add any carbs to the chicken.

- Boiled eggs - if you want next-to-no carbs, then this option should be on top of your list. Eggs are very nutritious and can be very helpful for your health. However, they still have a high protein level so you may need to eat them in moderate amounts.

- Canned fish like tuna, salmon or sardines. This can make the perfect addition to a salad that is low on carbs, and the oily fish is rich in omega 3 fats, and also has lower levels of protein than red meats. It seems to be the perfect meal for anyone on a keto diet.

- Coffee and many types of tea don't contain any carbs. However, you need to avoid additions like milk, cream, butter and obviously sugar. Using artificial sweeteners instead of sugar could still add some carbs. The only keto-approved natural sweetener is Stevia.

Pre- and Post-Workout Keto Snack Recipes

In order to have better positive effects, you will need to associate the ketogenic diet with an intense workout. The HIIT technique may be the right choice of physical exercise, which is an extremely intense workout during which you alternate heavy weightlifting with just a few seconds of break and then repeat the exercise for the same amount of time until reaching the state of exhaustion.

Usually, such exercises are preceded and followed by consistent meals, which are higher in proteins, and in some cases also higher in carbs. You will need all the energy you can get for such intense workouts, but you will also need a sufficient protein level to maintain your body mass. The fat level is still extremely high, and it should be because you need to burn the energy from the fat you consume. Remember, ketosis is a flexible metabolic state which allows you to play with the nutrient levels of your daily diet. Therefore, more carbs and proteins can be the right ingredients to make sure you perform at your best during these extremely intense exercises. Below, you can find some interesting keto snacks which are highly recommended on training days, before or after your training.

Pre Workout Keto Snacks

In this section, we outline a few wonderful keto snacks for the period before your workout, so you can get the energy you need and also make sure you have enough nutrients in your body to maximize the effects of your workout.

Pizza Bites

When you think of pizza, you automatically think of carbs, as a typical pizza is extremely heavy in carbs. However, keto pizza is a bit different, and can have really great effects on your energy levels before intense training. The crust (dough) is where the carbs are in a normal pizza. Well, the keto diet has found a way to make you forget you are not eating normal pizza. This kind of pizza only has 3 major ingredients: shredded mozzarella cheese (half a cup), a special keto marinara sauce (also half a cup) and 24 slices of sugar-free pepperoni. You only need to follow the simple steps below.

1. Turn on the broiler of the oven.

2. Place some parchment paper on a baking tray and lay out the pepperoni slices in a

single layer.

3. Put the keto-marinara sauce (1 teaspoon) on each slice of pepperoni and use a spoon to spread it out. Then add just a teaspoon of mozzarella cheese over the keto-marinara sauce;

4. Place the baking sheet in the oven and let it broil for about 3 minutes until you notice the cheese melting and turning slightly brown;

5. Take them out of the baking sheet and place them on a paper towel to absorb excess grease.

You can prepare around 6 portions, and each portion will have 82 calories, 5.4 grams of fat, 4.2 grams of proteins, 2.2 Carbs, Sugar 0.8 grams, and Fiber 0.3 grams.

If you are a big fan of Thai food, then the **Chicken Skin Crisps Satay** is right for you. This food can be the fat bomb and energy boost you need just before training. For this snack you will need coconut aminos (1 teaspoon), ¼ minced garlic clove, minced and seeded jalapeno pepper (1 teaspoon), coconut oil (1 teaspoon), unsweetened coconut cream (1 tablespoon) 2 tablespoons of chunky peanut butter (with no sugar at all), and the skin taken from 3 big chicken thighs.

In order to cook this meal, you will need to follow the instructions below:

1. Turn the oven on and heat it to 350 degrees Fahrenheit. In the meantime place the skins on parchment paper inside a baking tray. Make sure they are as flat as possible.

2. Place the baking tray with the skins inside the preheated oven and bake them for approximately 12-15 minutes, until you notice that the skins are crispy and light brown. You will need to monitor them properly, as you don't want to burn them.

3. Take the skins out of the baking tray and place them on a paper towel to cool.

4. Inside a small food processor, you will need to add coconut aminos, garlic, jalapeno, coconut oil, and peanut butter. It may take more than 30 seconds to properly blend, so make sure the mixture is smooth enough.

5. Every chicken skin has to be cut in 2 pieces, therefore there are 6 servings for this snack.

6. At this point you can put the mixture on the chicken skin, using a tablespoon. If your sauce is a bit too fluid, just place it in the refrigerator for about 2 hours, before spreading it on the chicken skin.

The chicken skin is extremely rich in fat, and before you put the skin to bake in the oven, you can simply drain the chicken fat off. This snack has 112 calories for each serving and it also 9.9 grams of fat, 3.8 grams of proteins, 1.6 grams of carbs, 0.2 grams of sugar, 0.6 grams of fiber.

Bacon and Garlic Dip

Luckily for you, the keto diet doesn't force you to renounce all of the foods you know and love. Many people enjoy eating bacon, but in many diets, bacon is a "no-no". The ketogenic diet, on the other hand, really encourages the consumption of bacon, as it's very rich in fat. This bacon and garlic dip is a calorie-dense snack, but it also has the right nutrients in it. The best part of this type of snack is that it can be combined with different keto- friendly veggies like celery and zucchini, or you can even try it with keto crackers made from flax meal.

For this special treat, you will need these ingredients: grated Parmesan cheese (half a cup), black pepper (half a teaspoon), 1 teaspoon of salt, 6 mashed and roasted garlic cloves, 1 tablespoon of lemon juice, chopped fresh parsley (2 tablespoons), full-fat Greek yogurt (¼ cup), full-fat sour cream (¼ cup), 8 ounce of softened cream cheese, 2 cups of chopped spinach, 8 slices of bacon (no extra sugar added). It sounds too delicious not to cook it.

Here's how to make it:

1. Start the oven and leave it on until it reaches 350 degrees Fahrenheit.

2. Use a pan or any kind of skillet to cook the bacon at medium heat, until the bacon becomes crispy. Take the bacon out of the pan and place it on a plate with paper towels in it to absorb the excess fat.

3. In the same pan, you will need to add spinach and to cook it until it becomes wilted. When wilted, you will need to turn off the heat and set the pan aside.

4. In a medium bowl, add pepper, salt, garlic, lemon juice, parsley, yogurt, sour cream, and cream cheese and beat them together until they all get combined and the mixture looks very smooth.

5. Chop the bacon and add it into the bowl where the mixture is. Add some spinach and Parmesan cheese, and then stir vigorously.

6. Transfer the whole thing to a baking pan and bake for around 30 minutes until it

looks hot and bubbly.

If you ever wondered how to roast garlic, here is a quick and basic recipe: "Roasting garlic brings out a deep flavor that you don't get with raw. Preheat your oven to 400°F. Remove the excess skin from 6 bulbs of garlic and cut 1/2" off the tips. Line a pie plate with aluminum foil and arrange bulbs in a single layer. Drizzle olive oil on top and wrap bulbs with foil. Roast 30 minutes. Allow to cool and remove cloves from the bulb. Store in the refrigerator up to 2 weeks."[3] This recipe is for 6 servings with 271 calories per serving, 20.4 grams of fat, 11.4 grams of protein, 5.3 grams of carbs, 2 grams of sugar and 0.4 grams of fiber.

One of the most appreciated keto snacks is **Jalapeno Poppers**. This snack is specially designated to spice up your diet--literally.

The ingredient list is not very long, either: 8 slices of bacon (sugar-free), 8 jalapeno peppers (medium), 4 ounces of softened cream cheese and half a cup of shredded pepper jack cheese.

---

[3] Boyers, L. (n.d.). *Keto Snacks From Sweet and Savory Fat Bombs to Pizza Bites and Jalapeno Poppers, 100 Low-Carb Snacks for Every Craving.* New York: Adams Media, p.53.

Sometimes you only need a few ingredients to create a masterpiece. Here's how to make this delicious snack:

1. Turn on the oven and heat to 425 degrees Fahrenheit. Prepare a baking tray with aluminum foil.

2. You will need to cut about a third of each pepper out lengthwise, to make room for filling. Take the seeds out.

3. In a small bowl, you will need to mix pepper jack cheese with cream cheese, then fill the peppers with the mixture. You have 8 portions of jalapenos to fill so you will need to divide the stuffing into 8 equal portions.

4. Cover each pepper in bacon, and place them on the baking tray. Put the tray in the oven and leave it to bake for approximately 15-20 minutes, until you will see the bacon crispy.

"The capsaicin in chili peppers is thermogenic, which means it generates heat by increasing the metabolism of adipose (fat) tissue. Eating capsaicin-rich foods may help stimulate the body's ability to burn fat."[4]

Post Workout Keto Snacks

For most diets, the meal after the workout should be such that it is able to compensate for the energy burned during the intense workout. Whether you are coming in after a long jog or swim, or after a really hard workout lifting weights at the gym, your body craves food, but you have to be very careful with the food you are consuming after training. Not only will the meal have to be rich in fats, but also in proteins, to uphold the muscle mass of your body. Some people enjoy consuming carbs after training, but with keto it is important to keep the carb consumption in check. This book already presented some of the downsides of eating too many carbs, so try to avoid them as much as possible, and when you are allowed to consume them, make sure you do it in moderation and use healthy foods to do so. You are probably wondering what the best foods to eat after training would be. The answer depends on variety of factors and will vary from one person

---

[4] Boyers, L. (n.d.). *Keto Snacks From Sweet and Savory Fat Bombs to Pizza Bites and Jalapeno Poppers, 100 Low-Carb Snacks for Every Craving.* New York: Adams Media, p.35.

to another, but below you can find some recommended foods and snacks to have after an intensive workout.

Prosciutto Chips

Although this is an Italian food, most people around the globe are familiarized with prosciutto because of people's love of Italian cuisine across the globe. In most cases, prosciutto is made from ham or the pig's hind leg. This type of meat is spiced without added sugar in most cases, so it's pretty keto-safe. It can be rubbed with salt, or it can be smoked. Prosciutto chips don't require an extensive shopping list, as you will only need two things for this snack: the oven and prosciutto. In order to prepare the food, you will need to:

- Turn the oven on and let it heat to 350 degrees Fahrenheit.

- Put some parchment paper inside a baking tray and then place the prosciutto slice by slice, to form a consistent single layer. Leave the tray inside the oven for about 12 minutes.

- After 12 minutes, the prosciutto should now be crispy, so it's time to turn off the oven and then let the meal cool off.

You can prepare food for 4 servings at a time, and each serving has 250 calories. Also, there are 19 grams of fat, 18 grams of protein and just 2 grams of carb per serving.

Another very delicious meal you can have after training is Taco Cups. This is a keto-friendly adaptation of the traditional Mexican food. Unlike the Prosciutto Chips, the ingredients list for this type of snack is quite long.

You will need Frank's RedHot sauce (3 tablespoons), chili powder (1 tablespoon), ground cumin (1 ½ teaspoons), ground paprika (½ teaspoon), 1 teaspoon of salt, 1 teaspoon of black pepper, dried oregano (¼ teaspoon), crushed red pepper flakes (¼ teaspoon), garlic granules (¼ teaspoon), onion granules (¼ teaspoon), 1 pound 75% lean ground beef, chopped cilantro (¼ cup), half of cup of salsa (sugar-free), 8 slices of sharp cheddar cheese (each slice should have 1 ounce). Here's how to prepare it:

1. Start the oven and heat it to 350 degrees Fahrenheit. Prepare a baking tray with some parchment paper.

2. In a small bowl, place all the spices and mix them together. You will need to use a pan or a medium skillet to cook ground

beef at medium heat. Please monitor how the beef is cooking in the pan because when it's almost done you will need to add the mixture of spices and stir to coat the meat entirely. When done, turn off the heating element and remove the pan from the stove.

3. At this point, you can place the cheddar slices in the baking tray. Leave them to bake for around 5 minutes, or until they start to get brown. Turn off the oven and then allow at least 3 minutes for the food in the tray to cool and then peel the parchment paper from the baking tray and take each slice aside and allow them to cool. You can put them at the muffin tin, just like a cup.

4. Take equal amounts of meat and place it into each cup and add a tablespoon of salsa sauce on top of them. Pour some hot sauce over it and also sprinkle some cilantro.

These taco cups have 457 calories per serving and this recipe creates 4 servings per batch. The nutrient breakdown per serving is: 32.2 grams of fat, 25.7 grams of protein, 5 grams of carbs, 1.5 grams of fiber.

Some people prefer a meal extremely low on carbs directly after they have finished their daily workout. A good option, in this case, should be crisps made from chicken skin with spicy avocado cream.

The list of ingredients includes: a half teaspoon of sea salt, half of a medium seeded and chopped jalapeno pepper, full-fat sour cream (3 tablespoons), a quarter of a medium avocado, pitted and peeled, and the skin from 3 big chicken thighs.

In order to make this keto food, follow these instructions:

1. Turn on the oven and heat to 350 degrees Fahrenheit. Prepare a baking tray with parchment paper and then place the skins on there. Make sure they are placed as flat as possible.

2. Place the tray in the oven and leave it to bake for about 12-15 minutes. When you notice the skins turning crispy and light brown, you will need to turn off the oven, as you don't want to burn the skins.

3. Take the skins from the baking tray and put them aside to cool, preferably on a paper towel.

4. Use a small bowl to prepare the cream. Add in the sour cream, avocado, jalapeno, and salt. Make sure the cream is properly and thoroughly blended.

5. Cut each crispy chicken skin in half.

6. Put cream on each piece of crispy chicken skin and then serve immediately.

This recipe is kind of similar to the Chicken Skin Crisps Satay, the main difference is the filling. There are also 6 servings, just like the other one, and each serving is low in calories, having just 86 calories. The nutrient breakdown is not bad either, having 7.5 grams of fat, 2.6 grams of proteins, just 0.7 grams of carbs, 0.4 grams of fiber and 0.2 grams of sugar.

Salmon and Lemon Fat Bomb

Salmon is known to be one of the most recommended type of fish you can have on this diet plan, just like tuna or sardines. This fish has a very well-balanced nutritional value, with a high concentration of fats, the right amounts of proteins, and very low carb counts.

For this specific dish you will need: a pinch of Himalayan salt, chopped dill (1 tablespoon), a tablespoon of lemon juice, smoked salmon (1.8 ounces), grass-fed butter (⅓ cup) and half a cup of cream cheese. In order to prepare this delicious meal, you will need to follow the instructions below:

1. You will need to add in a food processor lemon juice, dill, salmon, cream cheese and butter and blend them all together until you get a smooth mixture. Then add the salt and blend again.

2. Prepare a baking tray with parchment paper and put in the tray around 6 or 7 fat bombs (each fat bomb should contain 2 tablespoons of mixture). Use some more dill as garnish.

3. Place the whole tray into the refrigerator for about 2 hours, this should be enough time for the fat bombs to become firm, but not yet solid.

4. You can serve them when they are ready.

You can prepare 6 or at maximum 7 fat bombs, and each one have just 140 calories. As for the nutritional value, each fat bomb has 15 grams of fat (9 grams of saturated fat), 3 grams of protein and just 0.3 grams of carb.

Conclusion

The ketogenic diet can be one of the most effective treatments for conditions such as prediabetes, diabetes, heart, kidney and liver diseases, Alzheimer's and Parkinson's disease, and has also been shown to have a positive impact against slowing the growth of several types of cancer. With around 70% of the health conditions known today being caused by food, clearly something has to be changed in the way we eat, and most importantly in *what* we eat. Medication can encourage the body to react, or to mask the symptoms of diseases, to make the disease easier for the body to endure. This book proposes a different approach to preventing and even reversing these illnesses (if they are in such a phase which can allow reversal).

Being on a ketogenic diet is not always easy, especially at first, as you are radically changing the way you eat and what you eat. No good can come from consuming processed foods, as you will most likely end up with increased fat tissue, high blood sugar, and dysregulated insulin levels, leading to a predisposition for developing diabetes. Natural and organic food can be very difficult to find, as most products sold by supermarkets or other stores are becoming less and less natural and more and more processed. Modern farming involves using pesticides on fruits and vegetables, chemical fertilizers on grains and other plants, food concentrate on animals, before being slaughtered for meat. But you can change what you eat and how you eat it.

The basic principle behind the keto diet is eating a diet rich in fats and containing a lot fewer carbs, and moderation of protein intake. The main purpose of this diet is to activate the keto-adaptation process, a phase during which the body runs completely on fats, so it uses the fat reserves it already has and the fat you eat to produce energy for your body. Since you are depriving yourself of glucose because you are no longer eating carbs (or you are eating them in extremely low quantities), the body will only run on fats. The best part is, that if you work hard enough, the fats will not have the chance to get stored at all, and will be consumed immediately for energy.

The benefits of the keto diet are primarily for health, but many people use this kind of diet for fat loss and weight control. Just think about it! This is a guaranteed way to burn fats, so people with weight problems should consider this plan in order to lose weight. For better results, the diet should be combined with physical training in order to ramp up fat burning.

During the keto diet, the body will have a ketogenic metabolic state, allowing you to experiment with your macros in order to find the right way to do keto for *you*. I hope you have found this book and its included recipes helpful and informative, and that as you turn this final page, you feel excited and hopeful about beginning your new way of eating a new way of life. Thanks for reading, and enjoy taking your first step toward a healthier, happier you.

Bibliography

1. "60 Keto Snacks: Our Low Carb Snack Guide." *Nerd Fitness*, 25 Apr. 2019, www.nerdfitness.com/blog/50-keto-snacks-the-ultimate-low-carb-snack-guide/.

2. Boyers, L. (n.d.). Keto Snacks From Sweet and Savory Fat Bombs to Pizza Bites and Jalapeno Poppers, 100 Low-Carb Snacks for Every Craving. New York: Adams Media

3. Hendon, Louise. "The Best No Carb Snacks For Keto - Perfect For Your Diet!" *Keto Summit*, 30 Apr. 2019, ketosummit.com/no-carb-snacks-keto-low-carb-diet.

4. Mancinelli, K. (2018). *Jump Start Ketosis*. La Vergne: Ulysses Press.

5. Mawer, Rudy. "The Ketogenic Diet: A Detailed Beginner's Guide to Keto." *Healthline*, Healthline Media, 30 July 2018, www.healthline.com/nutrition/ketogenic-diet-101.

6. Munoz, Kissairis. "Keto Chocolate Avocado Pudding + 17 Other Keto Snacks." *Dr. Axe*, 29 Aug. 2018, draxe.com/keto-snacks/.

7. O'Neill, M. (2018). *Keto Fat Bombs Cookbook The #1 Low Carb & High Fat Snacks Cookbook for Ketogenic Diets, Lazy People & Weight Loss (5 Minute Fat Burning Keto Fat Bomb Recipes)*. Christopher Raymont

8. Spritzler, Franziska, and Andreas Eenfeldt. "What Is Ketosis? Is It Safe? – Diet Doctor." *Diet Doctor*, 22 Mar. 2019, www.dietdoctor.com/low-carb/ketosis.

www.ingramcontent.com/pod-product-compliance
Lightning Source LLC
Chambersburg PA
CBHW070122110526
44587CB00017BA/3176